for the

11+
NON-VERBAL
REASONING

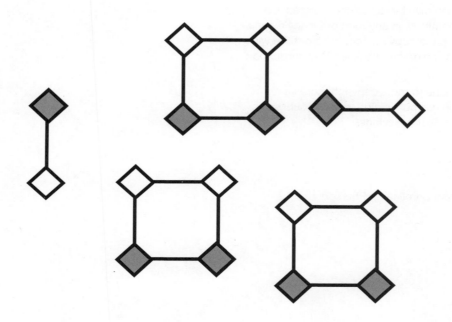

ges 10–11

ractice

Series editor Tracey Phelps,
the 11+ tutor with a

96% PASS RATE

📖 SCHOLASTIC

Published in the UK by Scholastic, 2020

Book End, Range Road, Witney, Oxfordshire, OX29 0YD

Scholastic Ireland, 89E Lagan Road, Dublin Industrial Estate, Glasnevin, Dublin, D11 HP5F

SCHOLASTIC and associated logos are trademarks and/or registered trademarks of Scholastic Inc.

www.scholastic.co.uk

© 2020 Scholastic Limited

1 2 3 4 5 6 7 8 9   1 2 3 4 5 6 7 8 9 0

A CIP catalogue record for this book is available from the British Library.

ISBN 978-1407-18378-7

Printed and bound by Replika Press Pvt. Ltd.

Paper made from wood grown in sustainable forests and other controlled sources.

Every effort has been made to trace copyright holders for the works reproduced in this publication, and the publishers apologise for any inadvertent omissions.

Author
Tracey Phelps

Editorial team
Liz Cremona-Howard and Caroline McPherson

Illustrations
Tracey Phelps

Contents

About the CEM Test

About the CEM test

The Centre for Evaluation and Monitoring (CEM) is one of the leading providers of the tests that grammar schools use in selecting students at 11+. The CEM test assesses a student's ability in Verbal Reasoning, Non-verbal Reasoning, English and Mathematics. Pupils typically take the CEM test at the start of Year 6.

Students answer multiple-choice questions and record their answers on a separate answer sheet. This answer sheet is then marked via OMR (Optical Mark Recognition) scanning technology.

The content and question type may vary slightly each year. The English and Verbal Reasoning components have included synonyms, antonyms, word associations, shuffled sentences, cloze (gap fill) passages and comprehension questions.

The Mathematics and Non-verbal Reasoning components span the Key Stage 2 Mathematics curriculum, with emphasis on worded problems. It is useful to note that the CEM test does include mathematics topics introduced at Year 6, such as ratio, proportion and probability.

The other main provider of such tests is GL Assessment. The GLA test assesses the same subjects as the CEM test and uses a multiple-choice format.

About this book

Scholastic 11+ Non-Verbal Reasoning for the CEM Test is part of the Pass Your 11+ series and offers authentic multiple-choice practice activities.

This book offers:

- Targeted practice and opportunities for children to test their understanding and develop their non-verbal reasoning skills.

- Opportunities to master different question types including similarities, rotation, codes, sequences, grids and more.

- Multiple-choice questions that reflect the different question types that are common in the CEM 11+ test, at a level appropriate for the age group.

- Short answers at the end of the book. Extended answers online with useful explanations at **www.scholastic.co.uk/pass-your-11-plus/extras** or via the QR code below.

Similarities

Find the shape that is most like the shapes in the box on the top left of each question. Circle one of the options A–F.

Example

A	B	C	Ⓓ	E	F

1

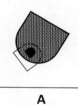	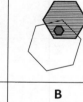				
A	B	C	D	E	F

2

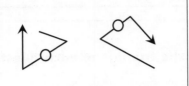

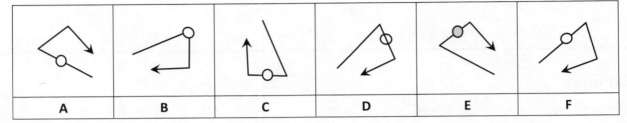

| A | B | C | D | E | F |

3

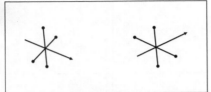

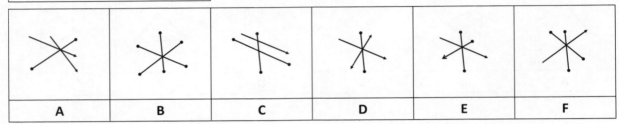

| A | B | C | D | E | F |

4

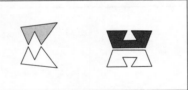

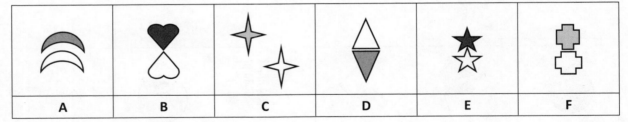

| A | B | C | D | E | F |

5

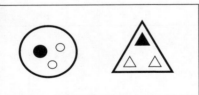

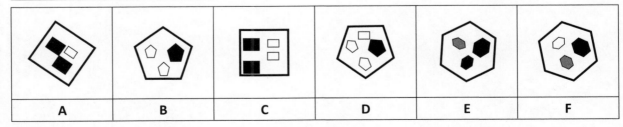

| A | B | C | D | E | F |

6

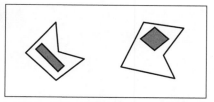

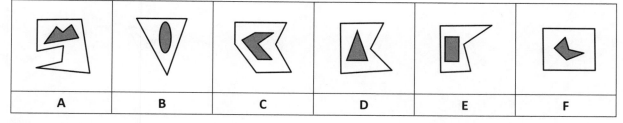

| A | B | C | D | E | F |

7

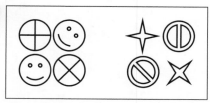

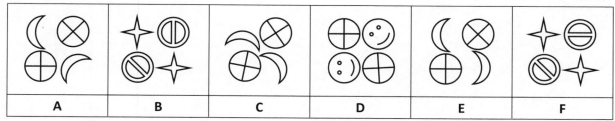

| A | B | C | D | E | F |

8

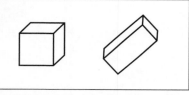

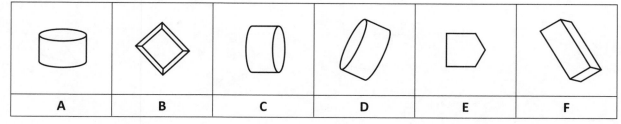

| A | B | C | D | E | F |

9

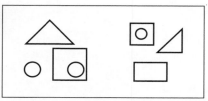

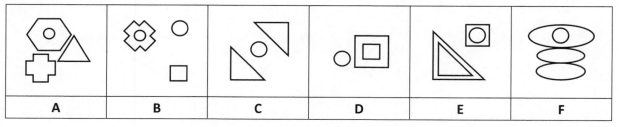

| A | B | C | D | E | F |

10

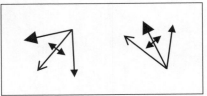

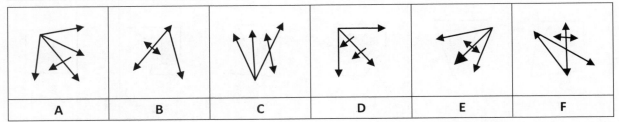

A	B	C	D	E	F

11

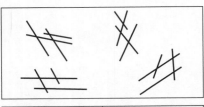

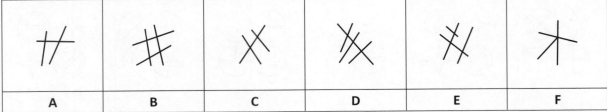

A	B	C	D	E	F

12

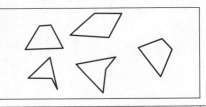

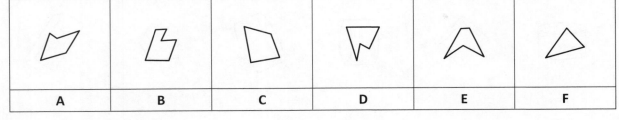

A	B	C	D	E	F

13

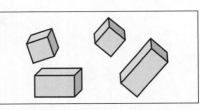

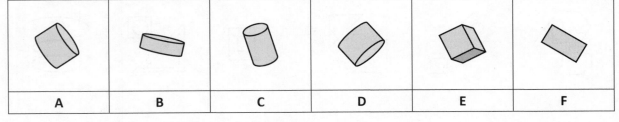

A	B	C	D	E	F

14

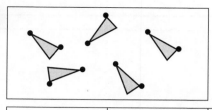

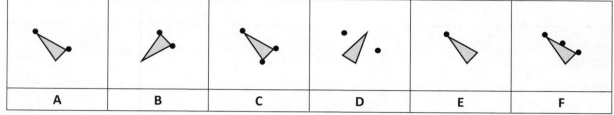

| A | B | C | D | E | F |

15

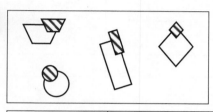

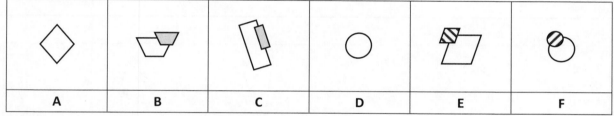

| A | B | C | D | E | F |

16

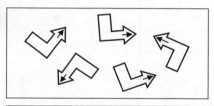

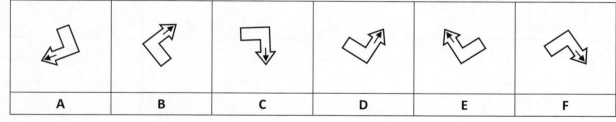

| A | B | C | D | E | F |

Differences

Which is the odd one out? Circle one of the options A–F.

Example

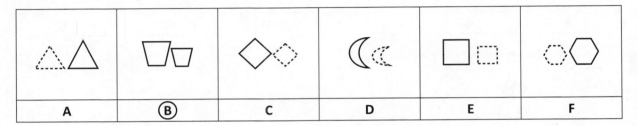

| A | B | C | D | E | F |

1

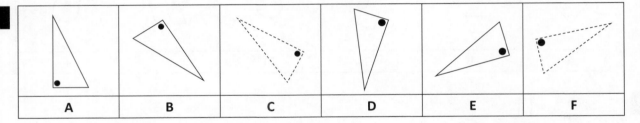

| A | B | C | D | E | F |

2

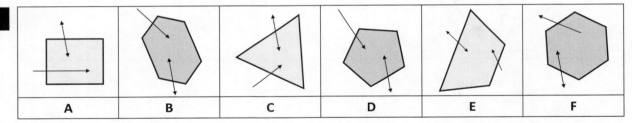

| A | B | C | D | E | F |

3

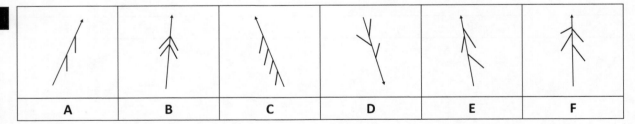

| A | B | C | D | E | F |

4

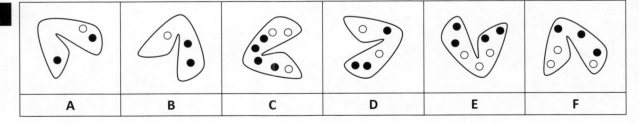

| A | B | C | D | E | F |

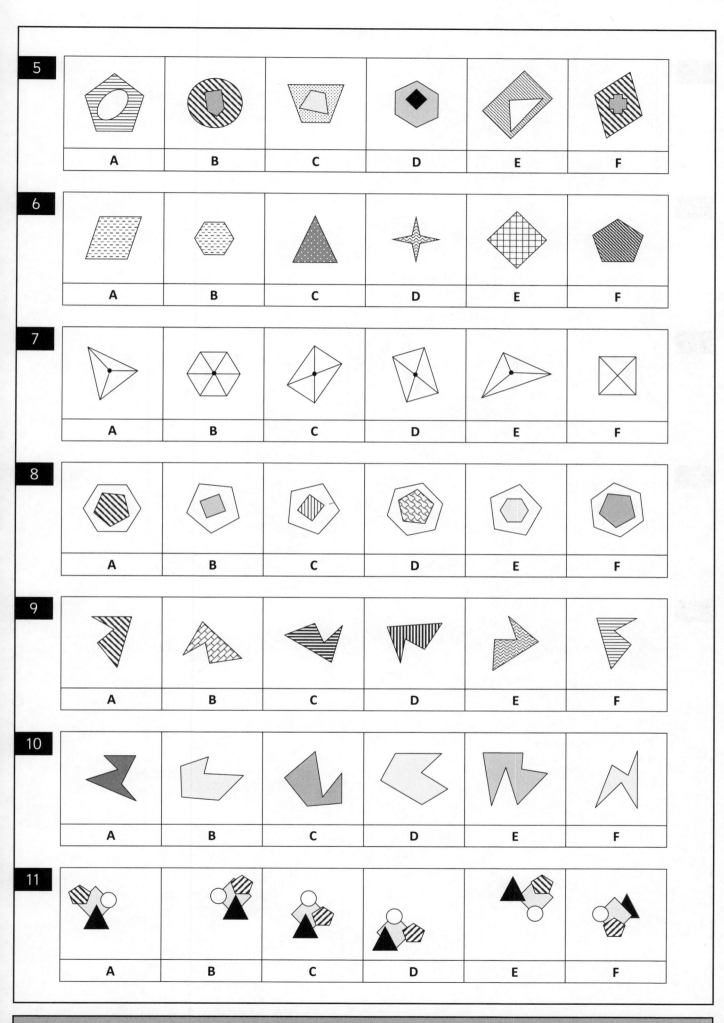

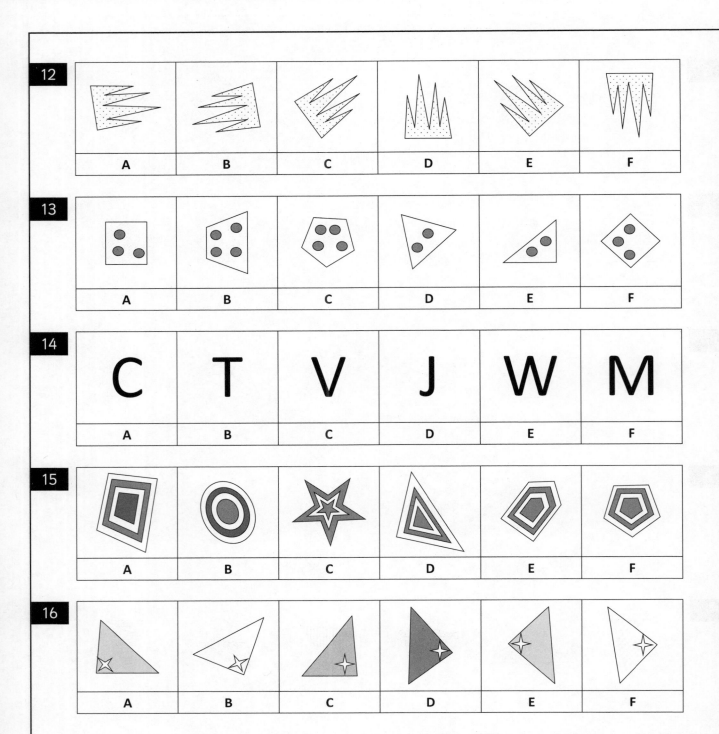

Analogies

The first two pictures on the left are related to each other in some way. Decide which picture is related to the third picture in the same way. Circle one of the options A–F.

Example

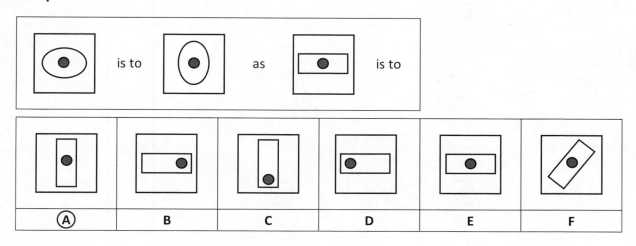

1

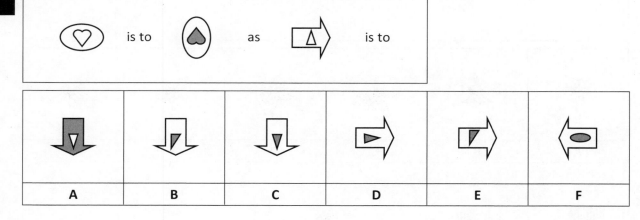

2

 is to as is to

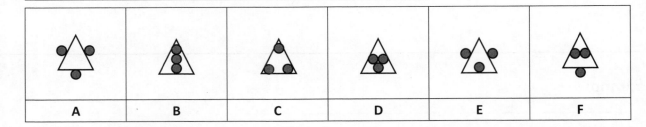

A	B	C	D	E	F

3

 is to as is to

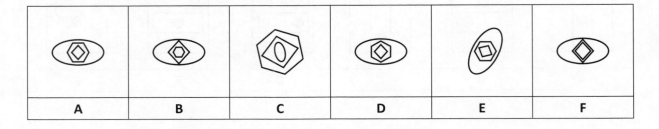

A	B	C	D	E	F

4

 is to as is to

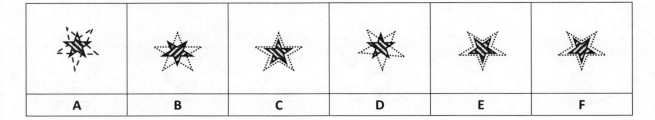

A	B	C	D	E	F

5

 is to as is to

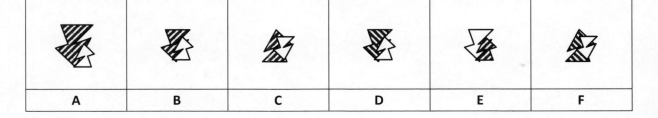

A	B	C	D	E	F

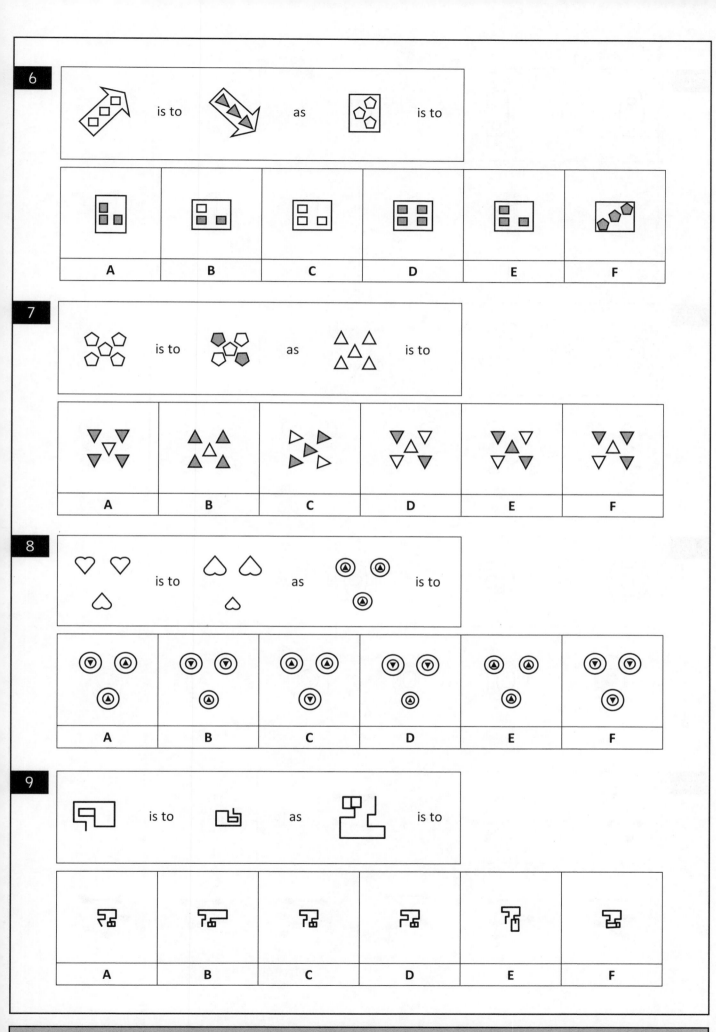

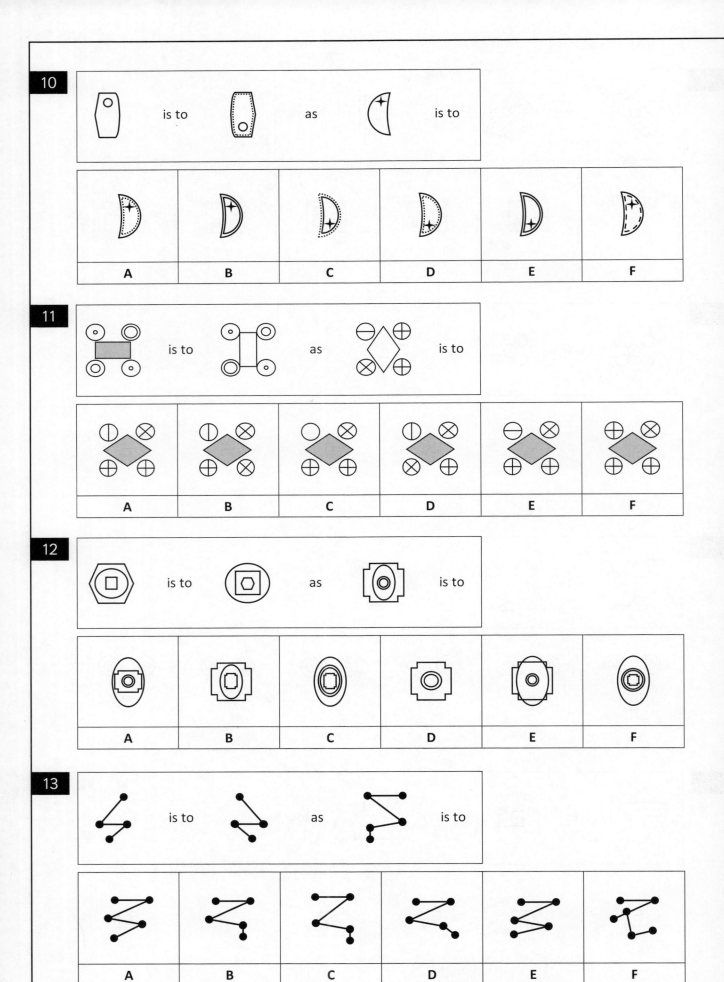

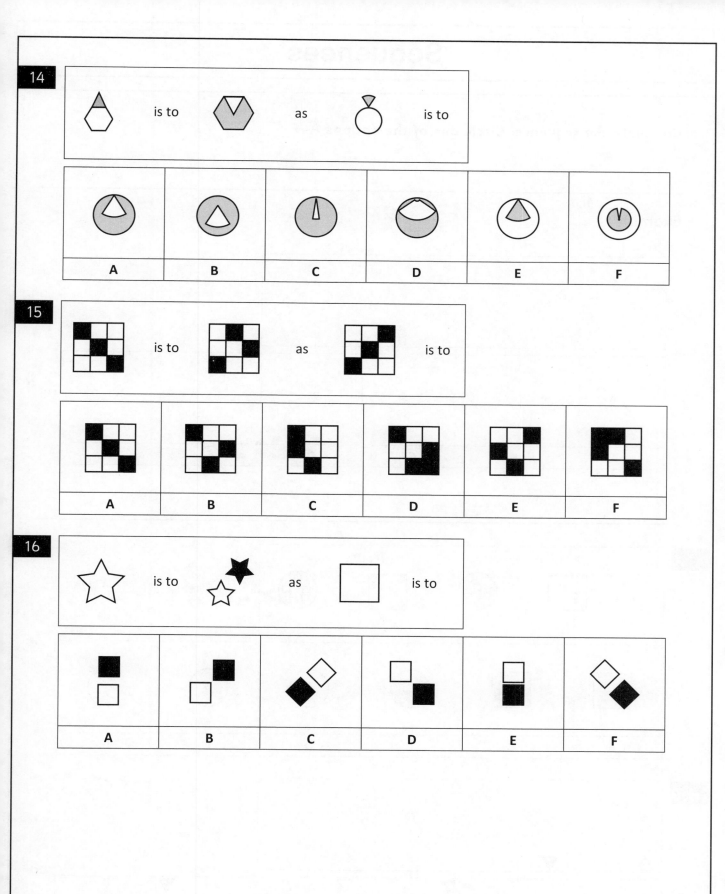

Sequences

Complete the sequence. Circle one of the options A–F.

Example

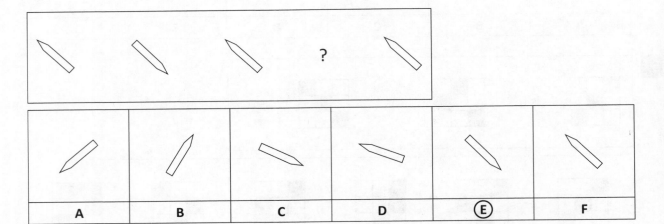

1

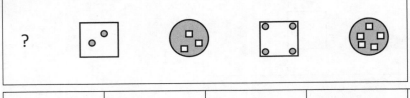

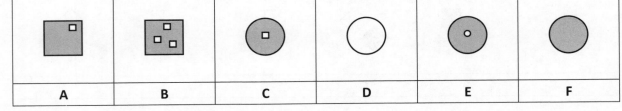

2

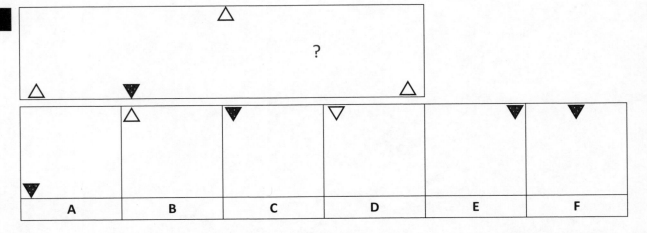

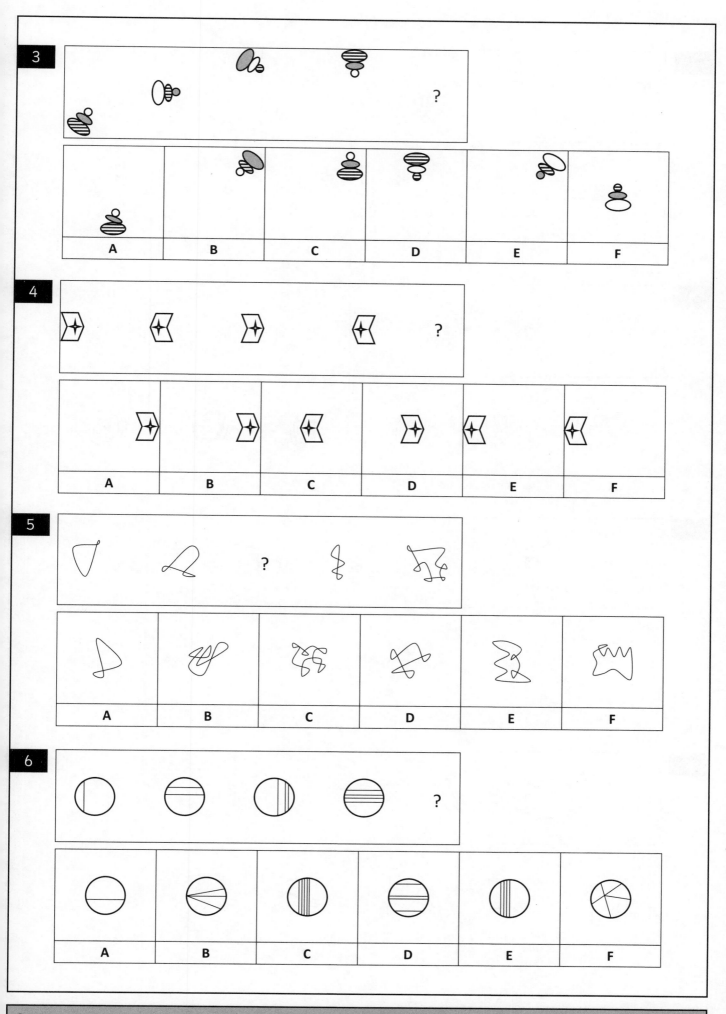

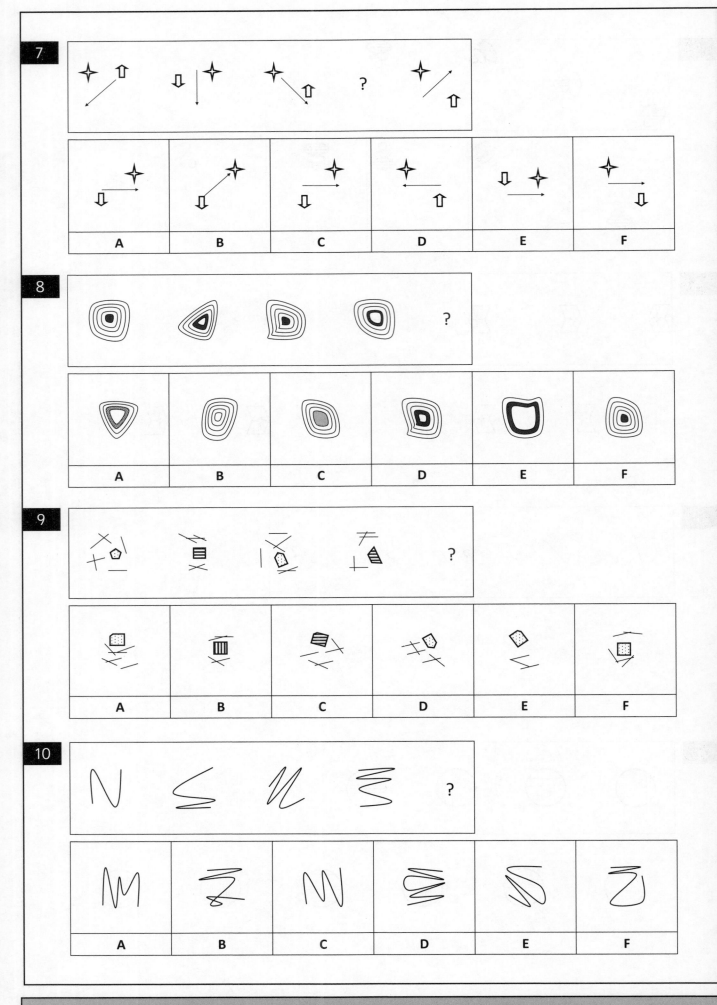

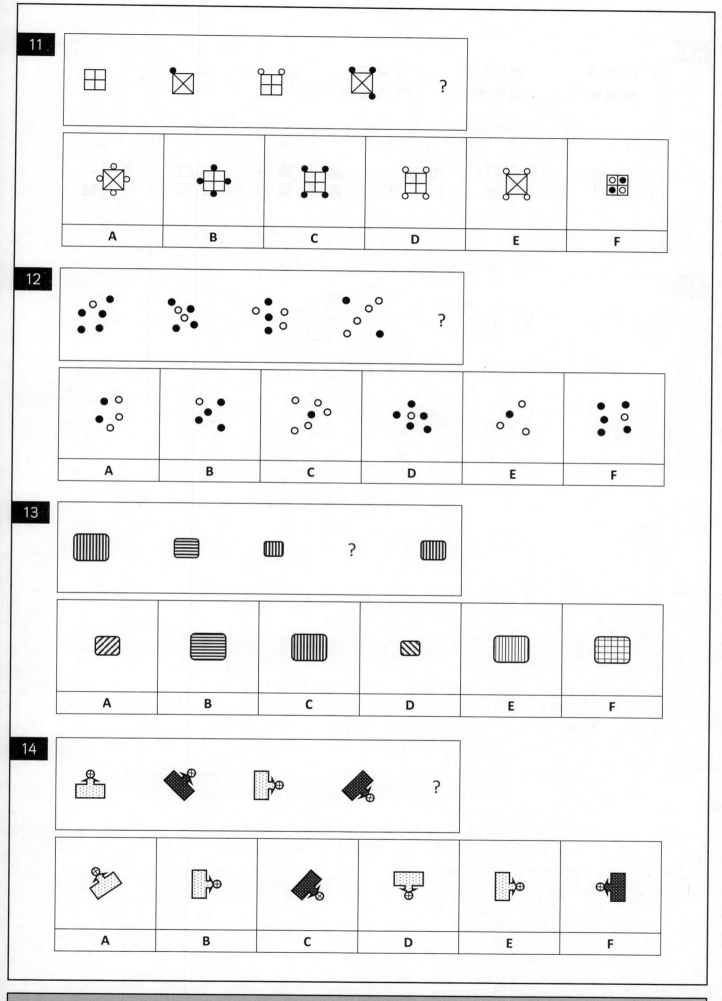

15

A	B	C	D	E	F

16

A	B	C	D	E	F

Grids

Find the correct shape to complete the matrices. Circle one of the options A–F.

Example

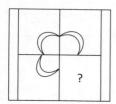

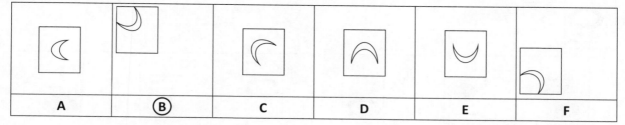

| A | B | C | D | E | F |

1

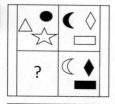

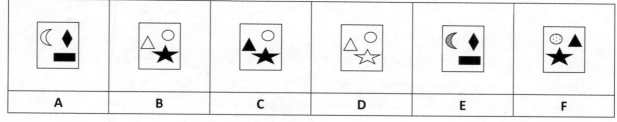

| A | B | C | D | E | F |

2

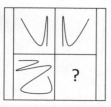

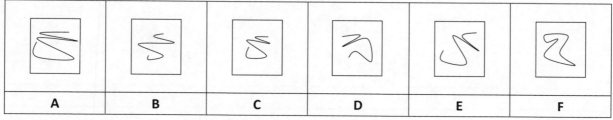

| A | B | C | D | E | F |

3

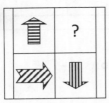

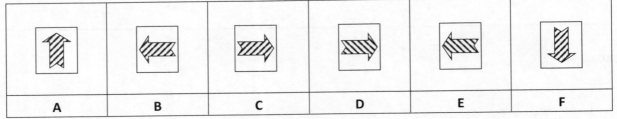

A	B	C	D	E	F

4

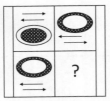

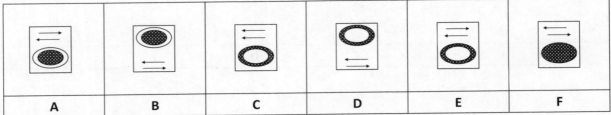

A	B	C	D	E	F

5

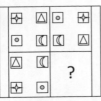

A	B	C	D	E	F

6

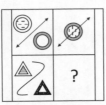

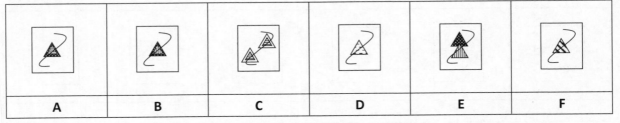

A	B	C	D	E	F

7

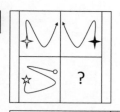

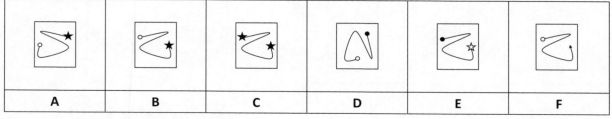

| A | B | C | D | E | F |

8

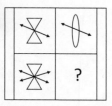

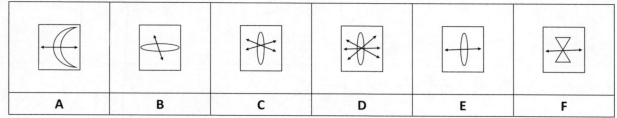

| A | B | C | D | E | F |

9

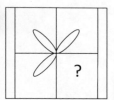

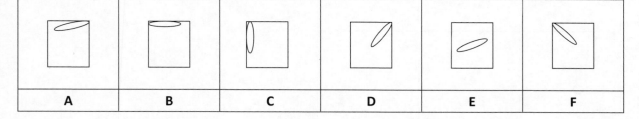

| A | B | C | D | E | F |

10

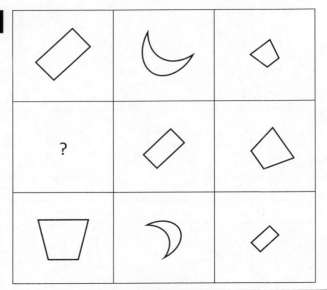

A	B	C	D	E	F

11

		?

A	B	C	D	E	F

12

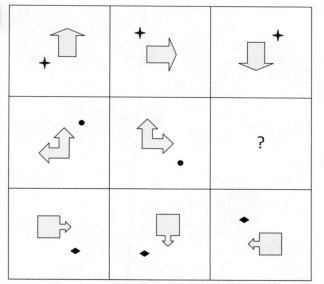

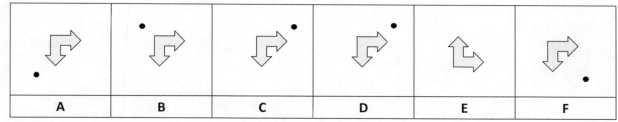

| A | B | C | D | E | F |

13

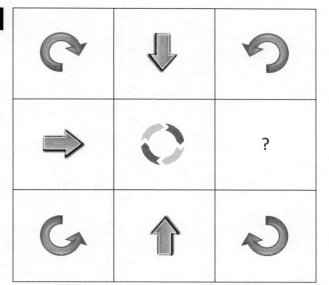

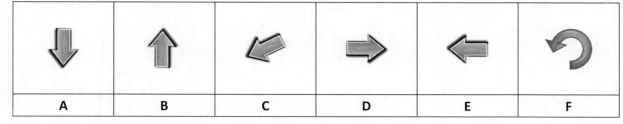

| A | B | C | D | E | F |

14

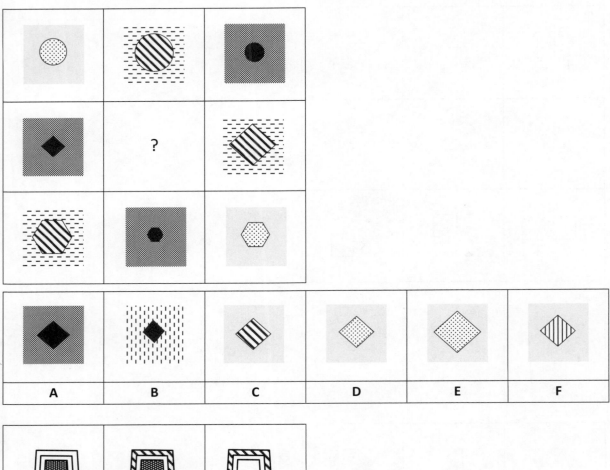

15

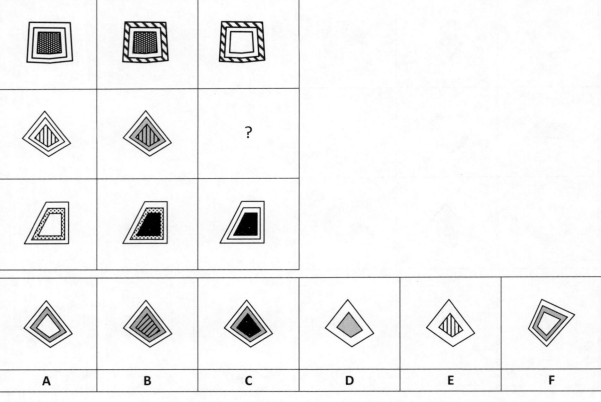

Rotations

Find the shape that can be rotated to make the top figure on the left. Circle one of the options A–F.

Example

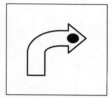

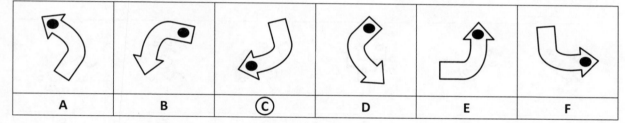

| A | B | Ⓒ | D | E | F |

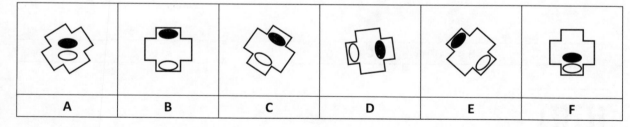

| A | B | C | D | E | F |

2

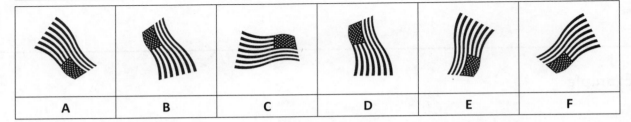

| A | B | C | D | E | F |

3

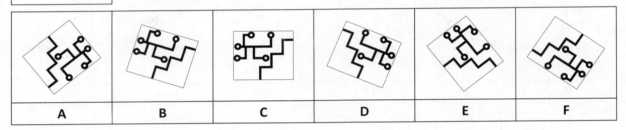

| A | B | C | D | E | F |

4

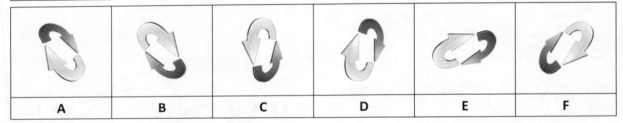

| A | B | C | D | E | F |

5

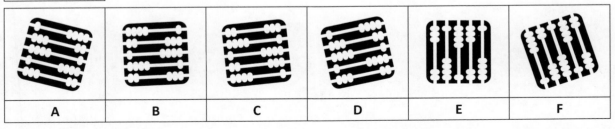

| A | B | C | D | E | F |

6

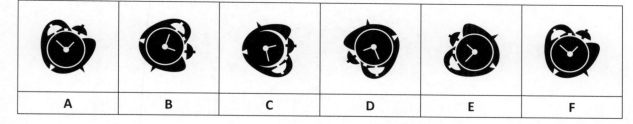

A	B	C	D	E	F

7

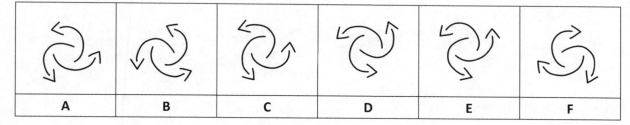

A	B	C	D	E	F

8

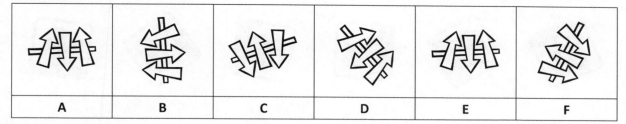

A	B	C	D	E	F

9

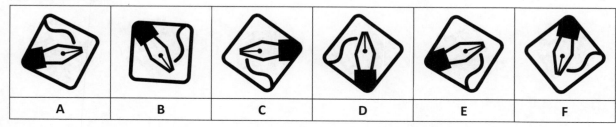

A	B	C	D	E	F

10

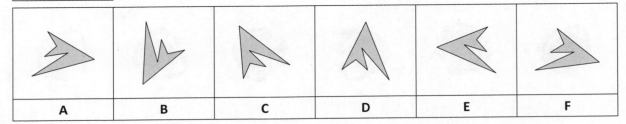

| A | B | C | D | E | F |

11

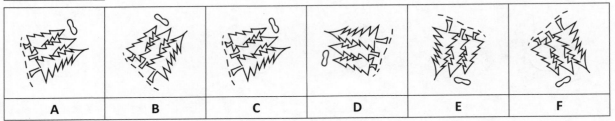

| A | B | C | D | E | F |

12

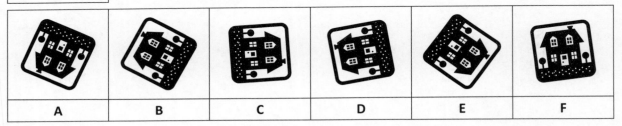

| A | B | C | D | E | F |

13

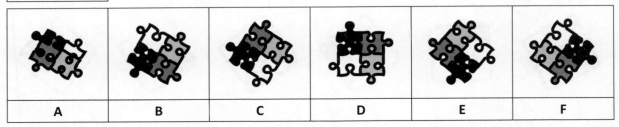

| A | B | C | D | E | F |

14

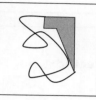

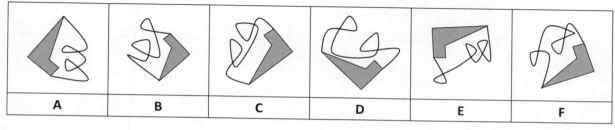

| A | B | C | D | E | F |

15

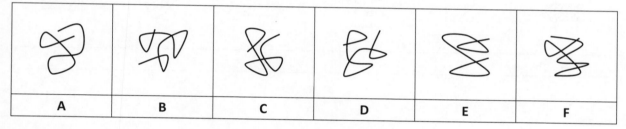

| A | B | C | D | E | F |

16

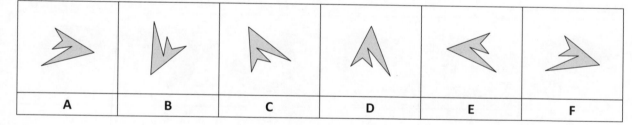

| A | B | C | D | E | F |

Reflections

Find the shape that is formed when the shape in the top-left box is reflected horizontally. Circle one of the options A–F.

Example

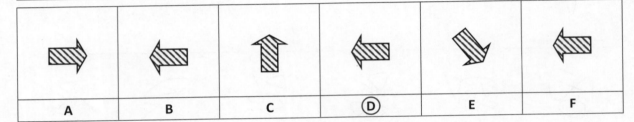

| A | B | C | D | E | F |

1

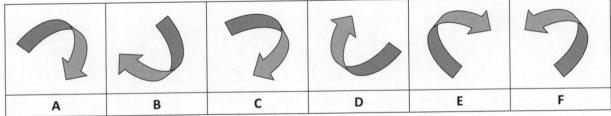

| A | B | C | D | E | F |

2

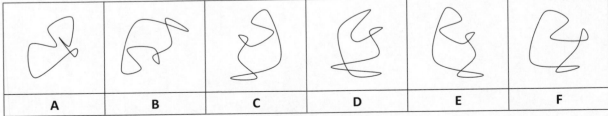

| A | B | C | D | E | F |

3

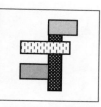

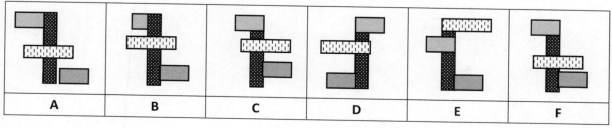

| A | B | C | D | E | F |

4

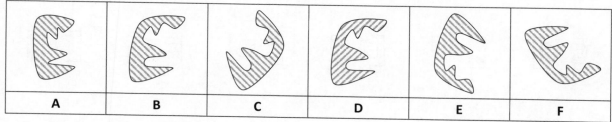

| A | B | C | D | E | F |

5

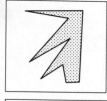

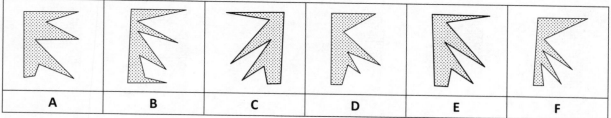

| A | B | C | D | E | F |

6

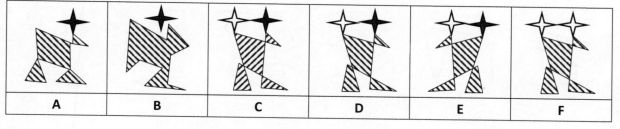

| A | B | C | D | E | F |

7

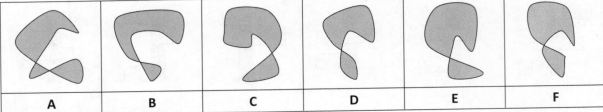

| A | B | C | D | E | F |

8

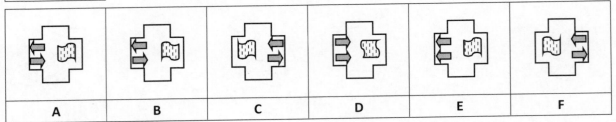

| A | B | C | D | E | F |

9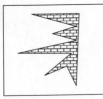

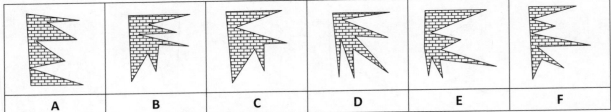

| A | B | C | D | E | F |

10

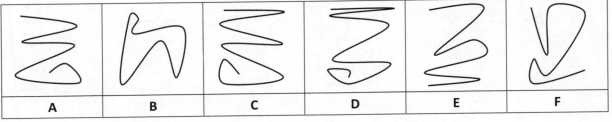

| A | B | C | D | E | F |

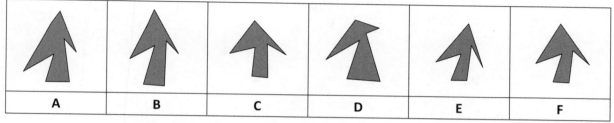

| A | B | C | D | E | F |

12

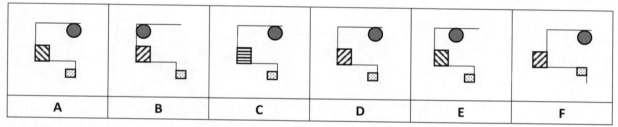

| A | B | C | D | E | F |

13

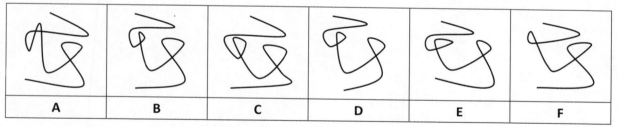

| A | B | C | D | E | F |

14

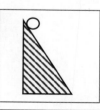

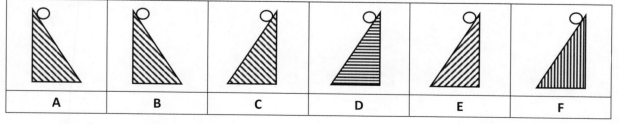

| A | B | C | D | E | F |

15

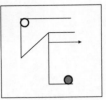

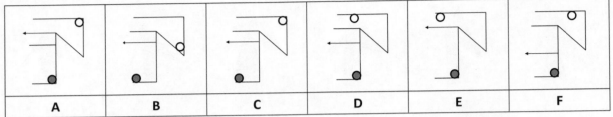

| A | B | C | D | E | F |

16

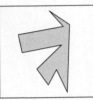

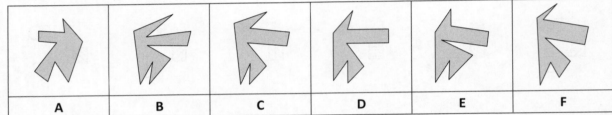

| A | B | C | D | E | F |

3D and Spatial Reasoning

Which cube matches the net? Circle one of the options A–F.

Example

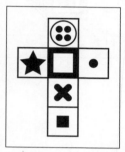

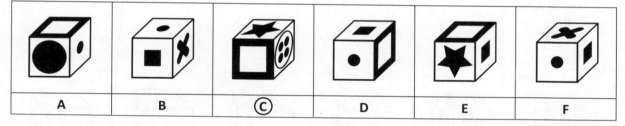

| A | B | © | D | E | F |

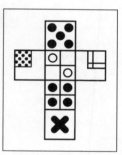

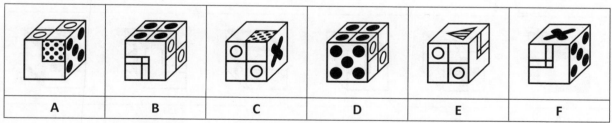

| A | B | C | D | E | F |

2

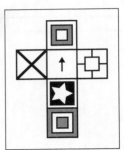

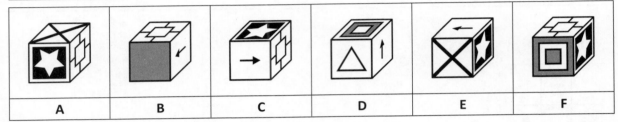

| A | B | C | D | E | F |

3

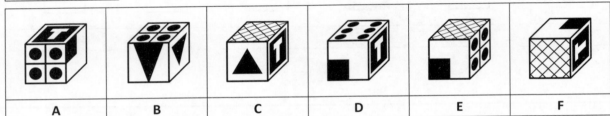

| A | B | C | D | E | F |

4

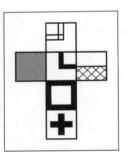

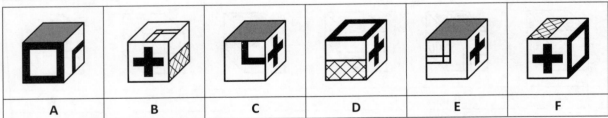

| A | B | C | D | E | F |

Which square creates the folded shape? Circle one of the options A–F.

Example

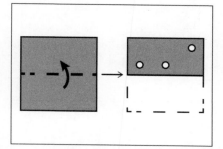

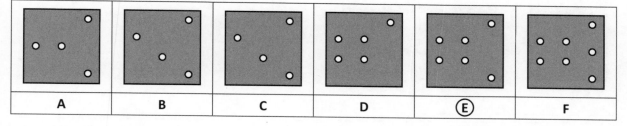

| A | B | C | D | (E) | F |

5

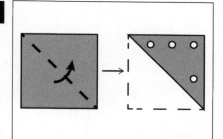

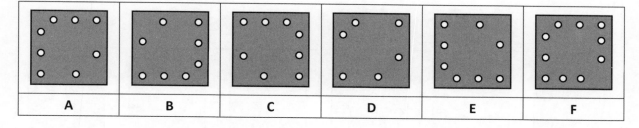

| A | B | C | D | E | F |

6

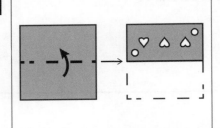

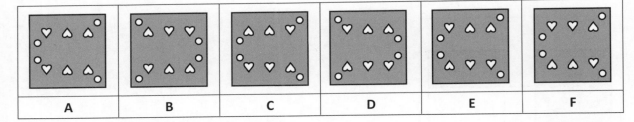

| A | B | C | D | E | F |

7

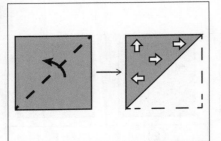

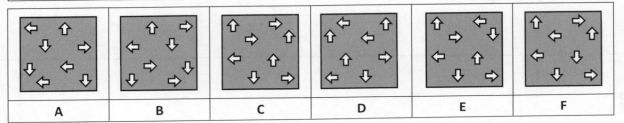

| A | B | C | D | E | F |

8

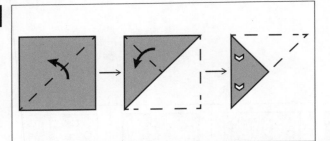

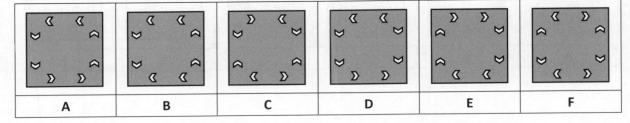

| A | B | C | D | E | F |

Which 2D plan matches the 3D view? Circle one of the options A–F.

Example

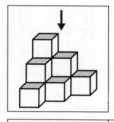

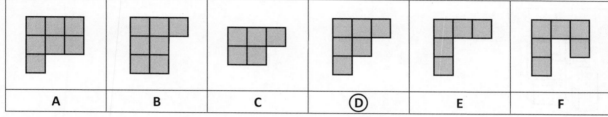

| A | B | C | Ⓓ | E | F |

9

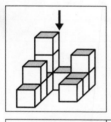

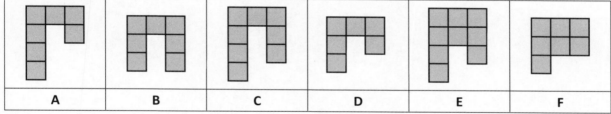

| A | B | C | D | E | F |

10

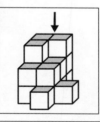

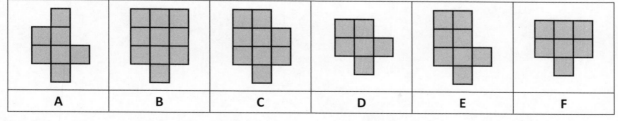

| A | B | C | D | E | F |

11

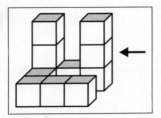

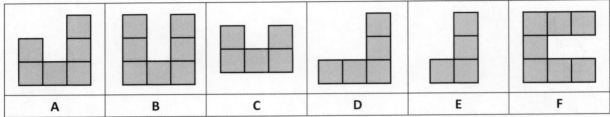

| A | B | C | D | E | F |

12

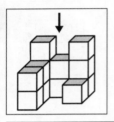

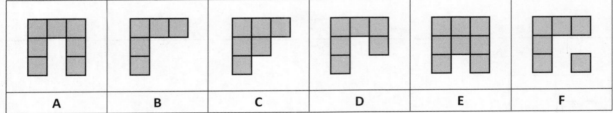

| A | B | C | D | E | F |

Codes

In the boxes on the left there are three shapes with code letters. Each letter describes one part of the shape. Work out what each letter is describing. Find the code that describes the shapes or patterns in the fourth box. Circle one of the options A–F.

Example

In the example, B describes the arrow pointing upwards and C describes the arrow pointing to the right. In the bottom boxes, L describes the pattern of stripes pointing to the right, M describes the pattern of stripes pointing to the left and K describes the pattern of black with white dots. Therefore the shape in the fourth box would be B and K.

Although the presentation of codes questions varies, the principle for finding the code remains the same.

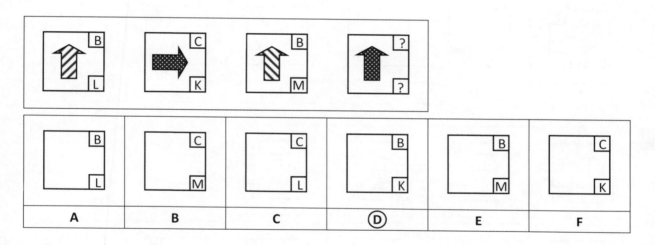

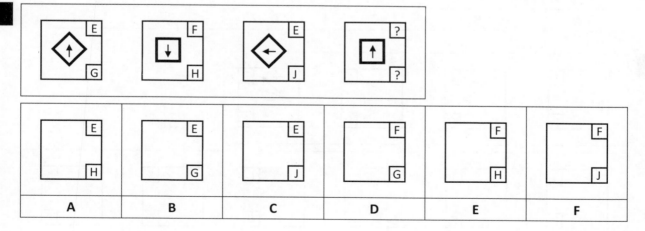

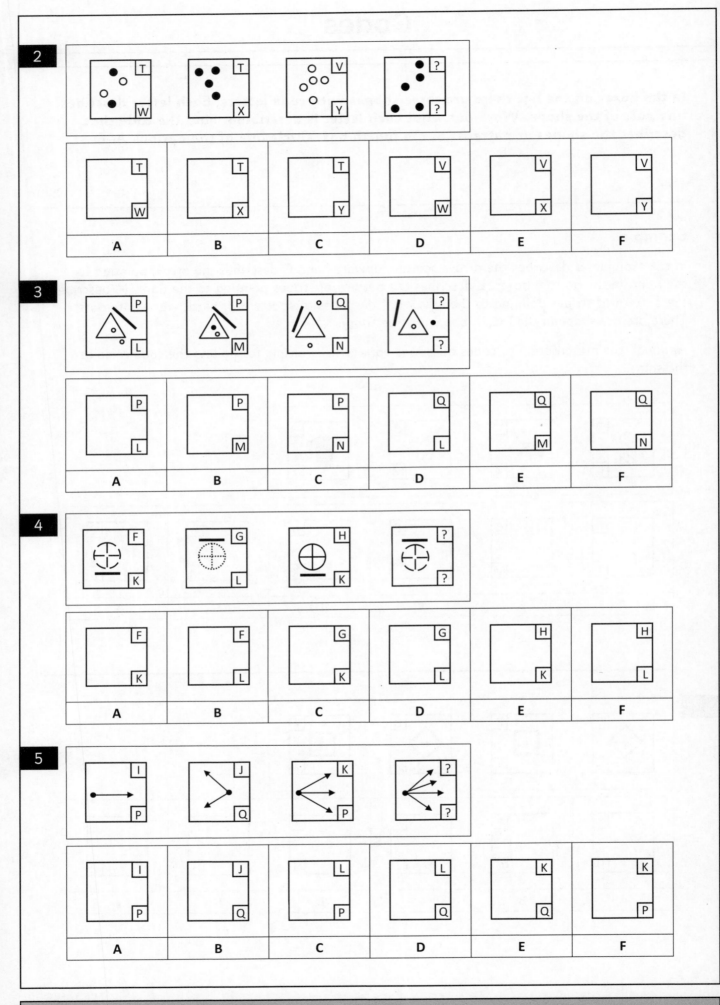

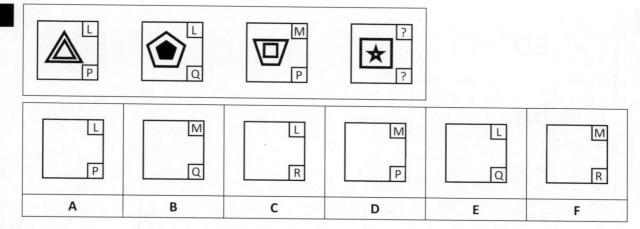

| A | B | C | D | E | F |

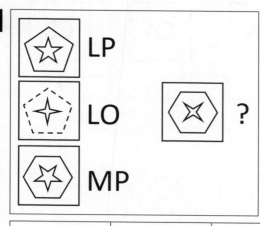

LO	MP	LP	MO	ML	LL
A	B	C	D	E	F

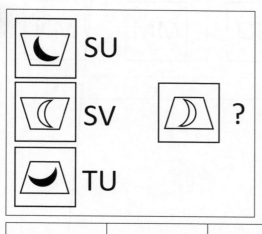

SU	SX	TU	TV	TS	TT
A	B	C	D	E	F

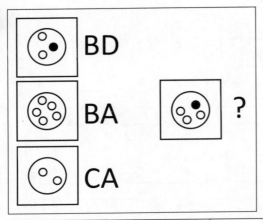

BB	CD	BD	BA	CA	CB
A	B	C	D	E	F

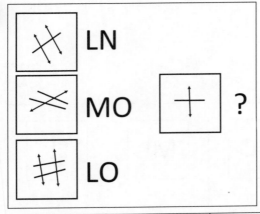

LO	LN	NO	MO	MM	MN
A	B	C	D	E	F

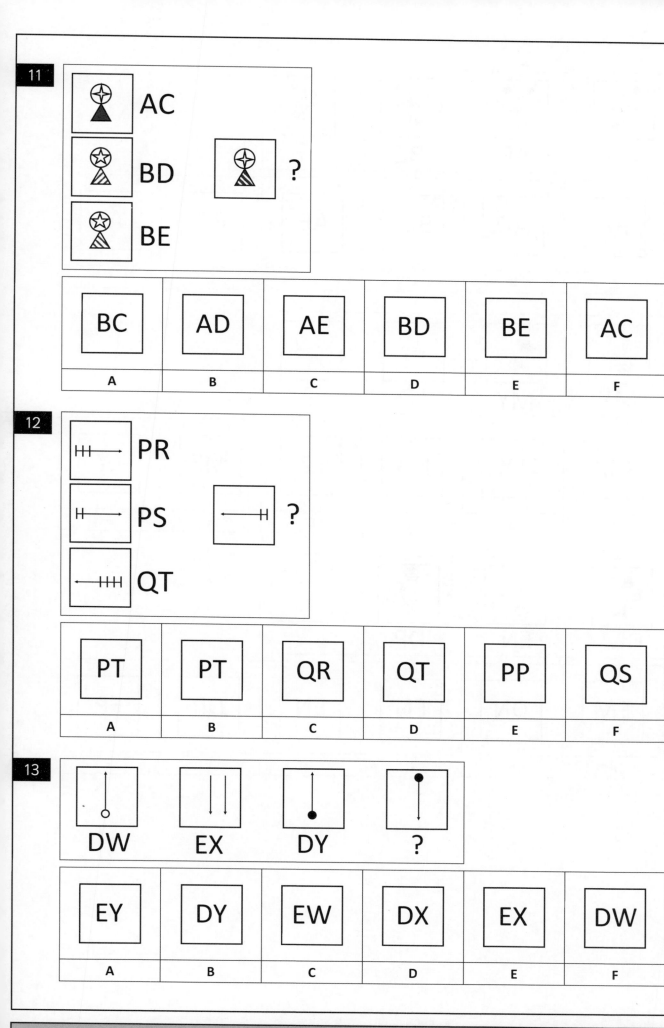

11

AC
BD
BE

?

BC	AD	AE	BD	BE	AC
A	B	C	D	E	F

12

PR
PS
QT

?

PT	PT	QR	QT	PP	QS
A	B	C	D	E	F

13

DW
EX
DY
?

EY	DY	EW	DX	EX	DW
A	B	C	D	E	F

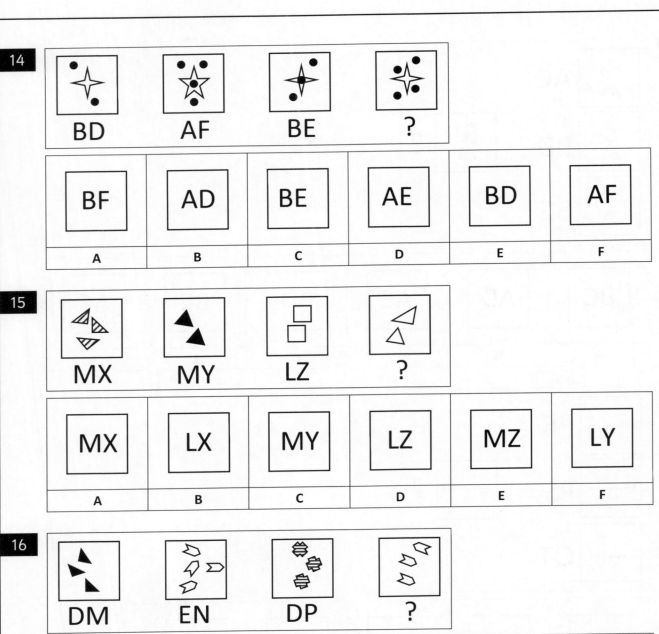

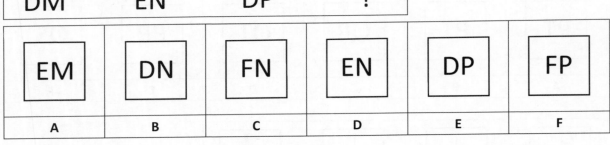

Mixed Test 1

For each question, circle one of the answers A–F.

1

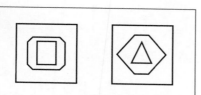

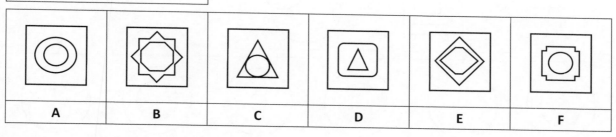

2

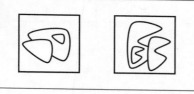

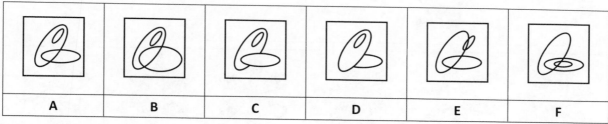

3

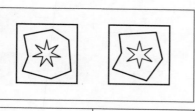

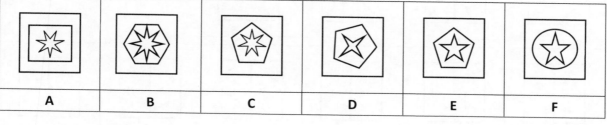

4

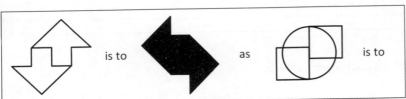

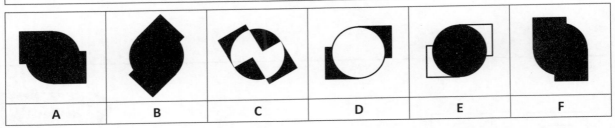

| A | B | C | D | E | F |

5

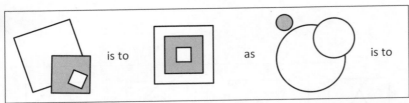

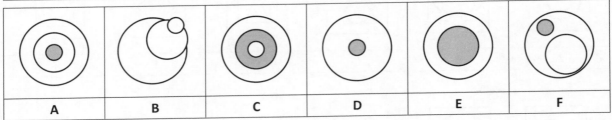

| A | B | C | D | E | F |

6

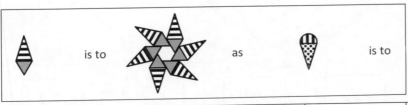

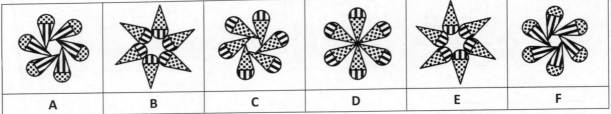

| A | B | C | D | E | F |

7

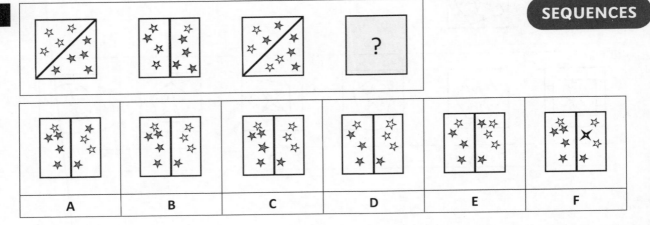

| A | B | C | D | E | F |

8

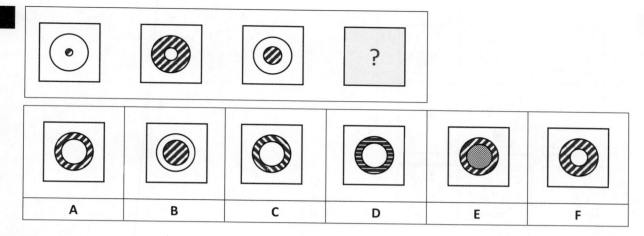

A   B   C   D   E   F

9

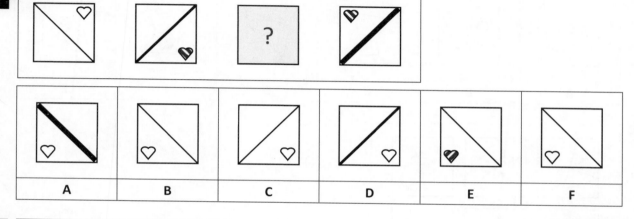

A   B   C   D   E   F

10

GRIDS

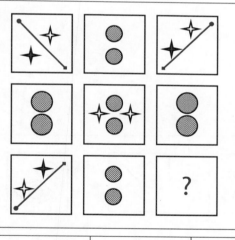

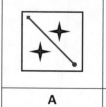   

A   B   C   D   E   F

11

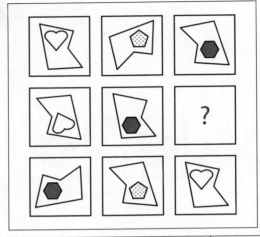

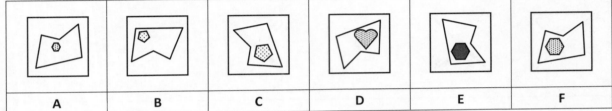

12

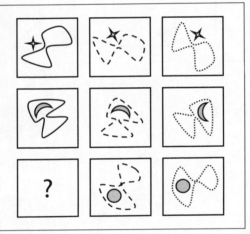

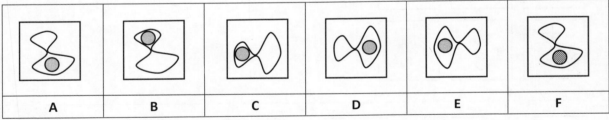

A	B	C	D	E	F

14

A	B	C	D	E	F

15

A	B	C	D	E	F

16

A	B	C	D	E	F

17

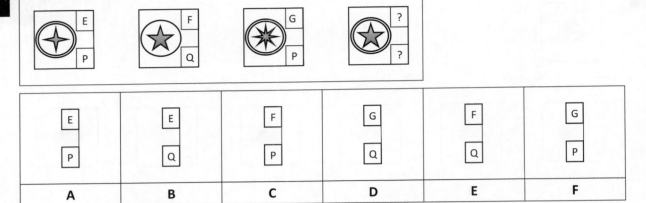

E	E	F	G	F	G
P	Q	P	Q	Q	P
A	**B**	**C**	**D**	**E**	**F**

18

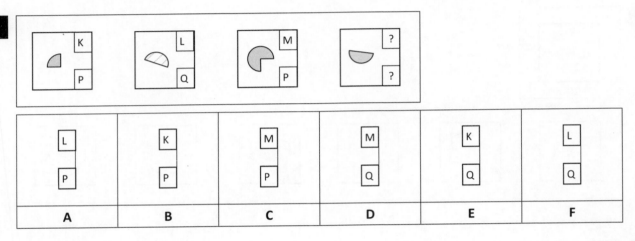

L	K	M	M	K	L
P	P	P	Q	Q	Q
A	**B**	**C**	**D**	**E**	**F**

Mixed Test 2

For each question, circle one of the answers A–F.

1

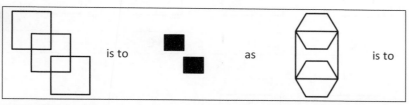

is to ... as ... is to

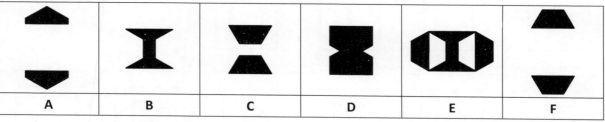

A	B	C	D	E	F

2

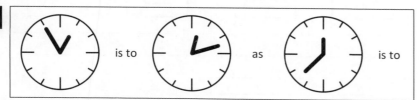

is to ... as ... is to

A	B	C	D	E	F

3

1 8
3 2 is to

9 2
  7 8 as

6
5 3 is to

	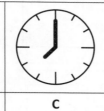	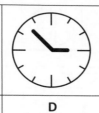			
A	B	C	D	E	F

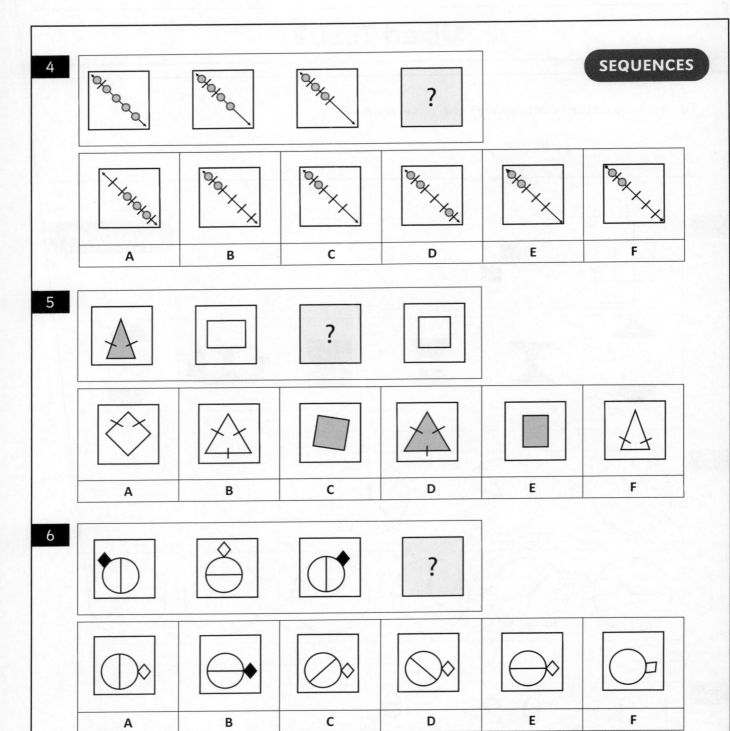

7

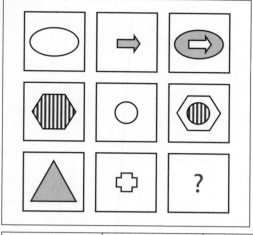

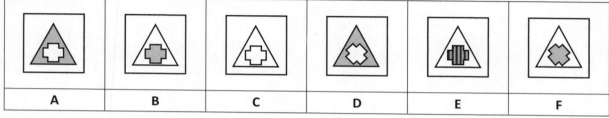

8

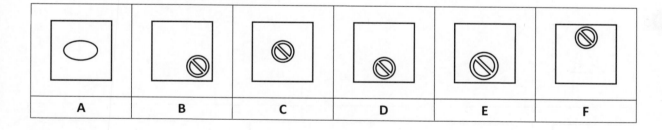

9

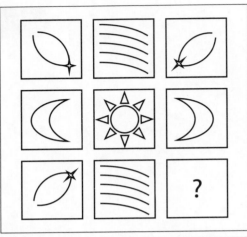

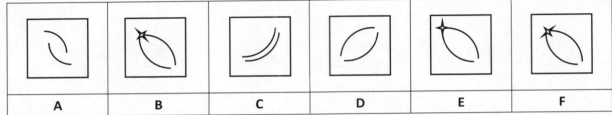

A	B	C	D	E	F

10

REFLECTIONS

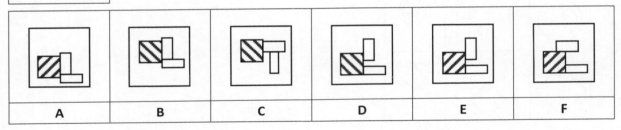

A	B	C	D	E	F

11

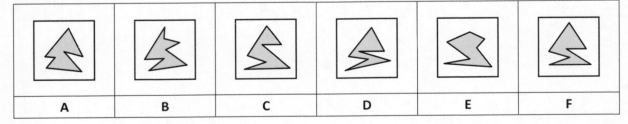

A	B	C	D	E	F

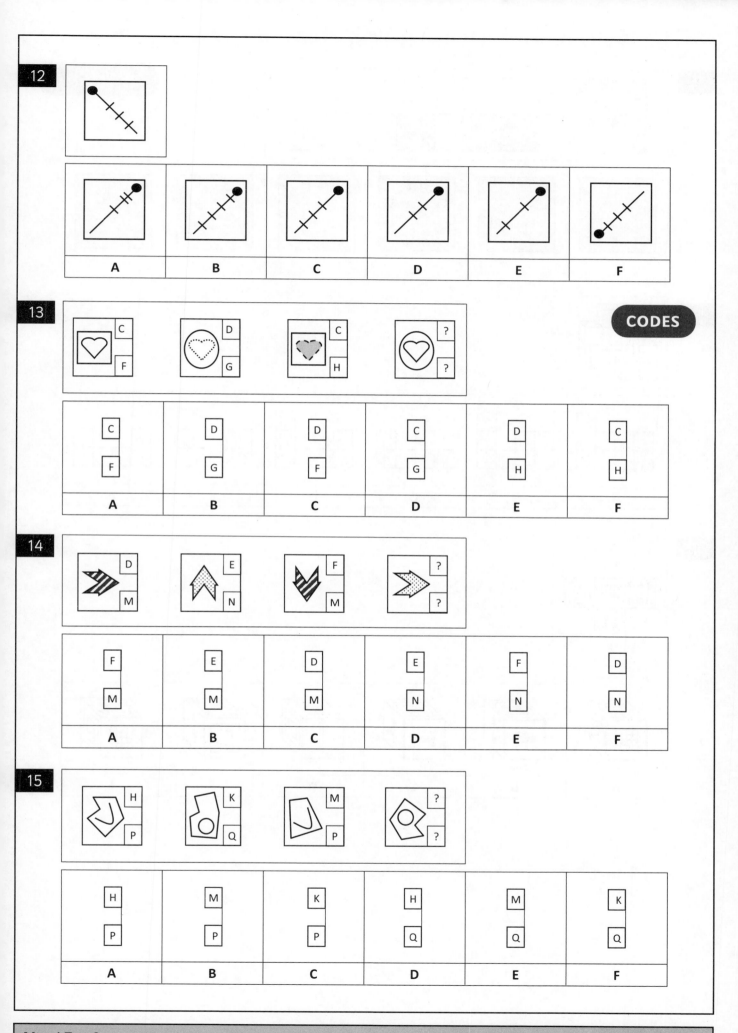

16

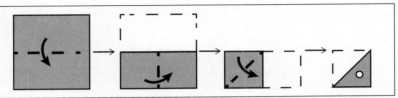

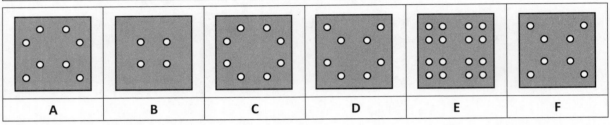

17

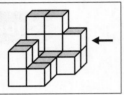

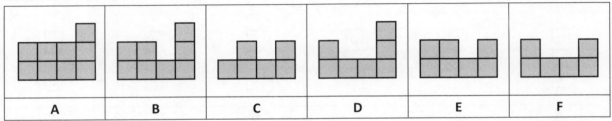

18

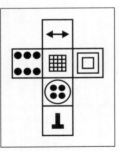

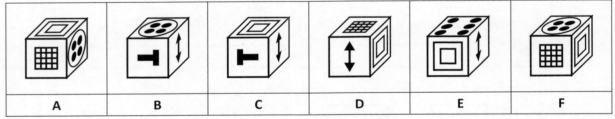

Answers

Extended answers with useful explanations are available online at
www.scholastic.co.uk/pass-your-11-plus/extras or via the QR code opposite.

Similarities
p.5

1	C
2	C
3	F
4	B
5	B
6	E
7	A
8	F
9	E
10	E
11	E
12	C
13	E
14	A
15	E
16	D

Differences
p.10

1	C
2	F
3	D
4	F
5	C
6	A
7	F
8	E
9	F
10	E
11	F
12	A
13	B
14	D
15	C
16	C

Analogies
p.13

1	C
2	D
3	A
4	F
5	D
6	E
7	D
8	B
9	C
10	D
11	E
12	F
13	C
14	A
15	B
16	B

Sequences
p.18

1	C
2	C
3	E
4	A
5	B
6	C
7	A
8	F
9	A
10	D
11	D
12	C
13	B
14	D
15	B
16	A

Grids
p.23

1	C
2	C
3	E
4	A
5	F
6	B
7	B
8	C
9	F
10	B
11	D
12	A
13	E
14	D
15	A

Rotations
p.29

1	D
2	A
3	D
4	C
5	B
6	C
7	F
8	B

9	E
10	E
11	F
12	E
13	B
14	D
15	D
16	E

Reflections
p.34

1	F
2	E
3	C
4	D
5	E
6	C
7	D
8	B

9	F
10	C
11	F
12	A
13	B
14	E
15	C
16	F

Answers

3D and Spatial Reasoning
p.39

1	B
2	E
3	B
4	A
5	A
6	E
7	C
8	E

9	C
10	E
11	F
12	D

Codes
p.45

1	D
2	E
3	D
4	B
5	C
6	D
7	D
8	D

9	B
10	F
11	C
12	F
13	A
14	A
15	E
16	B

Mixed Test 1
p.51

1	Similarities	B
2	Similarities	C
3	Similarities	E
4	Analogies	F
5	Analogies	A
6	Analogies	C
7	Sequences	E
8	Sequences	A
9	Sequences	F
10	Grids	E
11	Grids	C
12	Grids	A
13	Rotations	D
14	Rotations	D
15	Rotations	B
16	Codes	C
17	Codes	C
18	Codes	A

Mixed Test 2
p.57

1	Analogies	C
2	Analogies	E
3	Analogies	A
4	Sequences	C
5	Sequences	D
6	Sequences	E
7	Grids	B
8	Grids	D
9	Grids	E
10	Reflections	D
11	Reflections	F
12	Reflections	C
13	Codes	C
14	Codes	F
15	Codes	D
16	Spatial/3D	F
17	Spatial/3D	B
18	Spatial/3D	A